SO HIGH SCHOOL

ANA SHAY

Cover Design by Regan Kindrick

CHAPTER 1

Madison

His lips were on mine as he backed me into a quiet corner, only stopping when my I hit the cold concrete pillar. I pulled away from his mouth, giggling because his hand was tickling the back of my knee.

"Henry," I whispered so close to him, I could feel his breath against my lips. He traced his hand up my leg until it was playing with the hem of my skirt. "Someone could be watching."

Henry glanced down at my mouth, before rubbing his nose against mine. "Isn't that why we picked this place? Because no one is going to be looking for us here?

His hand was still on my thigh, sending tingles up my leg, and even though I knew he was right, the idea of anyone catching us with his hand up my skirt make me nervous. It didn't matter that we'd been meeting under the bleachers for the better part of six months because it was as far away from the hockey team as we could get, I always had this innate fear that my brother or one of his friends would find me.

Henry's hand skated a little higher up my skirt until he was palming one of my butt cheeks. I squealed backing into the cold, concrete pillar, trapping his hand in between.

"What are you doing?" I asked, clutching onto his shirt like it would help me stand.

He gave my ass cheek a little squeeze and raised his brow. "I don't know. I just thought that maybe I could take the opportunity to make you feel good."

"Feel good?" I asked with a high pitched voice. Swallowing down my nerves, I tried to make it look like I wasn't shaking like a leaf, and cursed myself for ever thinking I was ready or something like this. I might have been talking a big game to my cousin Tiff about wanting to have sex, but now that the opportunity was in front of me, I wasn't so sure.

Patting Henry on the chest, I looked down just as he kissed my cheek.

"I'm not sure I'm comfortable doing anything back here."

He slowly dragged his lips down my neck, and I instinctively tipped my head back, letting him leave a trail of kisses behind. Resting my head against the pillar, I closed my eyes, enjoying the tingling feeling it was giving me.

When his hand moved from my ass, I relaxed, until I felt his fingers toying with the waistband of my skirt.

I gasped and my hips bucked forward, which Henry took as a sign that I wanted this. I squealed the tiniest bit because yeah, it all felt nice, but did I want to be known as the girl who got fingered under the bleachers?

Just as one of his fingers tucked under the waistband, I heard footsteps and pushed Henry off me. Standing beside him, looking a little wrecked, I wanted to laugh because he had my lipstick smeared all over his face.

It was obvious what we were doing back here, and when a couple of seniors also looking for a little privacy came into view, I didn't know what to do.

"Sorry," I squeaked out and waved. Then inwardly groaned because did I really just do that?

Henry didn't even bother to look at the couple. He just scuffed his shoes across the concrete, leaving me to do all the talking.

"Are you guys still busy in here?" The girl asked, completely unbothered that she'd interrupted something.

"No. We're good." Henry mumbled.

Unfortunately, it was just as I said, "Yes. We'd like some privacy."

Cringing, I tipped on my toes then pointed with my thumb to the side. "I think the next set of bleachers is free. The last couple that were in there left with a bang a few minutes ago."

Without another word, the couple walked away, leaving me and Henry standing together. He didn't move to kiss me again, because apparently, whatever was on his shoe was more interesting.

Pulling his phone out, the smallest of smiles tugged at his lips.

"Who you talking to?" I asked in a desperate attempt to get his focus back on me.

His smile dropped when he glanced up for all of two seconds before he continued texting. "No one. My mom."

"So which one is it?" I was trying to be funny, but that didn't seem to help Henry's sudden change in attitude. He grumbled something, but I couldn't hear it.

Well, this was awkward.

I didn't know what to do or where to look because it seemed like Henry suddenly wasn't interested in talking to me, or even acknowledging my existence.

He sighed out, stuffing his phone back in his pocket and before he could say anything, I wet my lips and stepped toward him, ready to pick up where we left off. He stiffened in what I assumed was surprise when I leaned in to kiss him, and just as my lips were about to touch his, he turned his head, forcing my mouth to drag across his cheek instead.

Tiny wisps of hair grazed against my lips as I slobbered across his cheek. *This couldn't be happening.*

He was doing all he could to keep me away because he didn't want me to kiss him.

I was trying to be the sexy, cool girl, but failing miserably. So much so, that this was potentially the most embarrassing moment of my life

"What are you doing?"

His brows were crossed and if I hadn't just been kissing him, I would have thought I saw a little disgust behind his expression.

No more kisses. Even though we were alone.

Why did it feel like in the last few seconds I was being friend zoned?

Maybe I was over-thinking it. I did that a lot, and I'd never had a boyfriend before. Unfurling my arms from him, I backed away, nearly stumbling on my feet as I tried to think of something to say while hopefully calming down enough that my red cheeks weren't on show.

"I'm sorry, I just thought we weren't finished."

His lips remained tight, and it was the first time I thought he looked less than dreamy. With short, dark hair and hazel eyes, Henry was the kind of beautiful I only thought existed on the internet, so I couldn't believe my luck when he asked me out. Now I was starting to think my luck had run out.

"Hard to get back into it when you've been interrupted," Henry replied curtly.

He was being stand-offish, so I took another step back, not wanting to seem as desperate as I felt.

He was just kissing me, wasn't he?

"Henry, can we talk?"

Getting his phone out, he took another step away from me. When he saw whoever texted him back, that slight smile grew on his face again and I didn't know what to do. Was the person on the phone more interesting?

Fiddling with my hands, I wished I could say this was the first time that I was worried over Henry, but it wasn't. We'd been on shaky ground since we started dating. Well, I should say, I thought it was dating. Tiff didn't agree and had been suspicious since the first day I mentioned him asking me out. She was the only one that knew I was secretly seeing Henry because he'd asked me to keep it a secret from my brother.

"I'll have to figure it out later. I'm late for practice."

My brows came together in confusion because I knew that was a lie. Did he forget that my brother had the same schedule as him?

"Isn't practice in forty-five minutes?"

His head shot up, and he shook it vigorously.

"Yeah, but I need to do some pre-practice stretches before I go out there."

Still texting on his phone, I felt like asking him who was more important than me, but I didn't because I didn't want to know the answer.

"That's new," I said, doing a pretty crappy job of hiding my annoyance.

"Yeah, Dash has been trying to implement it with the team for a while now."

There was a little spike in my chest at the mere mention of my brother's best friend, Dash Bridges. The hot senior who I had one of those 'look but don't touch' kind of crushes on. You know the type. You look, but they don't *want* you to touch them.

I got it. I was the geeky little sister of his best friend, but I couldn't help by idolize him. Whenever he came over for dinner with our parents, I'd always try to come across as witty and cute, but no amount of interesting facts would get him to look up from his plate. I'd always have a little soft spot for that guy, but right now, he was inadvertently getting in my way.

"He does love to stretch, I guess," I said sarcastically, and Henry nodded.

"He also doesn't like it when we're late, so I'm sorry to do this, but I've got to go."

I took a sharp breath, masking my disappointment with a smile because Henry didn't look all that sorry about leaving me.

Henry gave me a peck on the check as he turned to leave. "I'll speak to you later."

My knees shook as I watched him walk out, because, for some reason, it felt like the end. I knew it in my heart, I was just hoping seeing him might have changed his mind.

Biting my bottom lip to stop myself from crying, I walked out of the bleachers and squinted when the sunlight covered my face. I pulled my phone out of my pocket, only to see a message from Tiff.

Tiff: Where are you? I thought we were having lunch together.

Shaking my head, I swiped out of her message because I told her this morning that I was meeting Henry. She even gave me that sassy tut of hers because she thinks I'm wasting my time with him.

Tiff and I had plans, and unlike my brother who was a star athlete, the only way we were getting into Covey U or Southern Collegiate was through our grades. Boys shouldn't have been that much of an interest to me. Especially boys who were on my brother's team, but I couldn't help myself, I seemed to be drawn to them.

Without really thinking, I sent a quick message to Henry because the way we ended things didn't feel right.

Madison: Good to see you today. Hopefully, we can catch up a little more next time.

"Shit," I whispered to myself, because my text reeked of inexperience and desperation. It wasn't my fault. I just didn't know how to act around guys and my behavior was proving that. I stuffed my phone in my pocket, refusing to reread it, knowing that it would only work me up into a bundle of anxiety.

So instead of standing around, I decided to find Tiff and headed to the lunch hall, shaking off all my nerves.

When I opened the door and caught eyes with Tiff, her face lit up.

I wanted to go and join her, but the stark reality of seeing Cade and Dash eating their lunch together with the rest of the team confirmed what I didn't want to admit.

Henry lied.

He wasn't with them, and that shouldn't have been a surprise because I didn't think they even liked each other, but I was still stunned, confused and a little dejected after my conversation with Henry. Seeing his lie was only making it worse.

Tiff figured I was upset without me having to say a word, and I saw her excuse herself from the table. As she headed straight toward me, I didn't want our friends seeing how upset I was, so I walked outside. By the time I reached my locker, she had caught up and placed her hand on my shoulder.

"There you are!" Tiff said, pulling me into a side hug. The minute I felt my cousin's arms around me, the strength that was keeping me together started to crumble.

He left me. He didn't want me. He never did.

It was pathetic to be thinking like this, but something felt off. Something wasn't right between me and Henry. Tiff squeezed harder, and when she pulled back, she cupped my cheek and wiped away an errant tear with her thumb. "Not here. Not in the hallway."

She was right. I didn't want everyone knowing my business, especially because that meant it would get back to Cade.

"Is this about Henry?" She whispered.

I silently nodded, sucking in a harsh breath. "Yeah, I, uh, don't think he's really that into me."

She sighed, but didn't say anything. I knew it was because she never thought we were dating in the first place, but I was glad she wasn't gloating or throwing the fact that she was right in my face.

"We were kissing under the bleachers, and I think we were heading into the territory of doing a little more, but then we got interrupted. After that, he was just on his phone and told me he was too busy to stay."

With her hand on my arm, Tiff rubbed her thumb against my shirt, giving me a look that dripped with so much sympathy, I wanted to tell her to stop, but I felt too broken to even try.

"Who knows? Maybe he was?" I looked at Tiff with disbelief, surprised that she was standing up for him.

"Uh, he told me he was going to practice but I know that was a lie because he said something about Dash wanting to do pre-stretches."

"Where's the lie in that?"

"Dash doesn't like people on a good day, and I know for a fact, he likes to stretch alone." I looked down at my shoes, not willing to look at her when I said, "There's also the fact that Dash and Cade were just in the lunch hall, most definitely *not* stretching."

Tiff bit her bottom lip, taking it all in. "Well if he lied, he's an asshole, and next time I see him in the hall, I'm going to trip him up."

"No. don't do that."

"Why not?"

"Don't hurt him on my account. If you do, then he'll know I told you, and that will make things worse."

"Wait, do you still *want* to be with him?"

I tried to hide my embarrassed smile because I couldn't answer that truthfully without sounding desperate. Maybe I was? No one had ever looked at me the way Henry had, and I had this innate fear that no one ever would again.

"I don't think he's done anything wrong. I think there's just some miscommunication going on between us."

"I don't think it's that."

My mind flitted to every conversation and every kiss we shared, noting something very absent from our interactions. Something that he was trying to rectify right before he got so standoffish.

"Do you think he's acting weird because I'm a virgin?"

Tiff's brows crossed. "We're sixteen. Aren't we all virgins?"

"I don't know. I just kind of thought teenage guys like girls that put out, and I've not really given him any signals that it's something I'm interested in."

"*Are* you interested in it?"

"I, I don't know."

"Then don't let your first time be with an idiot who doesn't know if he wants to be with you or not." Her words sounded simple, and I knew logically that was how I should feel, but for some reason, I just didn't.

I looked down to the floor, studying my spotless Mary Janes again. It was the only reason I could think for why Henry would have suddenly left me.

I did say I didn't want to do anything in the bleachers. Did he take it that I didn't want to do anything at all?

Biting my bottom lip, I gained up enough courage to say, "It's not like that. It's just, after six months, we haven't gotten past kissing."

Tiff stepped back to take me in fully. "You're not serious, are you?"

"Uh."

Raising her hand, she stopped me from saying anything else. "You're telling me that you're considering losing your virginity to a guy that seems more interested in Dash's foam roller than you because you've only made out with him?"

I shrugged because, when she put it like that, it made me feel small. I rolled my shoulders, looking down the hall toward the front doors, fully expecting Henry to walk through them and wrap me in his arms, telling me he was in a bad mood and that he was sorry. Then he'd kiss me in front of everyone.

But then I frowned because that would never happen. We'd have to actually tell people we were dating but that wasn't something he was even willing to entertain. He'd shown no interest in seeing me past our weekly bleachers meet up.

Sneaking around and trying to hide our relationship from my brother sounded fun at first, but it was starting to complicate things.

"That's not the only reason I want to lose my virginity. In two weeks, it's the start of summer vacation and we'll be heading into our junior year. I don't want to be left behind."

"And who exactly are you leaving behind? I've not had sex," She said, tilting her nose up, and clutching onto her textbooks like they were her lifeline. Tiff was my best friend. Always had been since we were little, but my goodness, she had no idea how to have a good time. At the start of high school, I was right along with her. I had buck teeth and resembled a bean pole back then. It was only after my braces came off, and my mom took me to get highlights that I started to yearn for a life outside of studying.

I hated to say it, but I changed, and along with that, things changed between Tiff and me. We wanted different things. I wanted to date, and kiss boys. She seemed more interested in reading the next chapter of her latest fantasy book, and that was fine, but it made it hard for us to relate.

"It's different when you don't want it." I didn't know what else to say. I looked in both directions, making sure everything was clear. "The thing is, I think he's worried I'm not ready."

"If you're not, then don't let him force you into it."

I shook my head. "He wouldn't be forcing me into anything. I think I'm ready, too. It's just never been the right time to talk about it with him. We're usually too busy making out."

"Pfft," She pushed out, stopping herself from laughing. "Do you even like Henry that much? No offense, but whenever you're in public, you completely ignore each other."

"That's because he wants to keep it a secret."

"From who? Cade?"

I winced as I nodded. The mere mention of my brother's name had the uncanny ability to sour the mood.

"Not just him. It's the entire hockey team. He doesn't want any of them thinking he's dating me to try to get into the popular hockey crowd."

Tiff stared at me with wide eyes, silently assessing me.

"Are you serious?"

"Yeah?" I looked around; the hallway was quiet as most people had headed to the hall for lunch. "What?" I said so loudly that the noise reverberated against the lockers.

"Do you seriously believe that? Because Madison for a girl that is so smart, I can't help but feel like you're so dumb sometimes."

"What are you talking about?"

"It's been six months. He doesn't want to be seen with you in public, he doesn't want to tell anyone about you, he only makes out with you under the bleachers. Do you guys even talk?"

I bounced on my toes, a little unsure of how to respond. Tiff really did know how to cut me down when she wanted to.

"It's because-"

"Because. Because. Because. I hear you giving him a lot of excuses for what I'd say is pretty shitty behavior."

"It's just, what if it's me?"

"What do you mean?"

"What if it's because I'm clingy and insecure and have been pushing him too much?"

"You see him alone under the bleachers once a week. I wouldn't say you're pushy," She snorted out a laugh, but it was no comfort to me. I still felt like I was doing wrong and that I could fix him.

I tried to smile, but it dropped quickly, and when I took a breath that somehow inadvertently turned into one of those sniffle cries.

Crap. I was this close to crying in the hallway about a secret boyfriend, and it was starting to feel pathetic.

"Hey, Mads. If that idiot doesn't want you because you haven't offered yourself up to him yet, then he's an asshole and doesn't deserve you."

She wrapped her arm around my shoulder, pulling me in as we walked down the hallway. I kept my head down, not wanting to draw attention to myself. Not that I ever did.

"You're fantastic, and one day you'll find someone that deserves you. Someone that is so obsessed with you that they'll burn down cities just to see you smile."

"I'd settle for a guy that would just tell people he likes me."

"You'll get that. I promise. Now come on, let's go to the bathroom and touch up your make up."

I nodded, still not sure what to do or where I stood with Henry, but not feeling confident enough to go out there and ask him outright.

Mainly because I was worried about the answer.

Dash

"California," My best friend and forever teammate, Cade drawled out before he snaked his arm across my neck to bring me in. He raised his hand and looked to the sky as we walked out of the lunchroom. "We're going to be in California in less than three months, playing hockey and attending the college of our dreams. Can you believe it?" I turned and rolled my eyes. He was smiling eagerly, so I shrugged him off, and moved away.

"Considering we applied to the same colleges, then, yes, surprisingly, I can believe it."

He pushed me on the shoulder, chuckling. "Grumpy as shit still. Come on. You can't deny that you're happy that we're one step closer to being brothers for life?"

"You're acting like we've just discovered we're going to the same college when we've known for months."

"That's because we are two weeks away from graduating. You and me.

It's Covey U to start, but who knows what the future holds for us." He raised his brows. "Maybe we'll even end up on the same NHL team."

"Let's focus on actually getting drafted before worrying about the team we're on." I was still nervous even mentioning it. Cade and I had been invited to attend the Draft live, which showed that several teams were looking at us, but that still wasn't a guarantee we'd get drafted. We could just as easily end up one of those players sitting in the arena, faking a smile because we weren't chosen just in case the camera panned on us.

"How does Amy feel about you moving to California?"

I shook my head and huffed out an annoyed breath. "I don't think she cares."

"Really?"

Shrugging, I adjusted my backpack on my shoulder. "She's staying here, and I'm moving away. It's kind of a moot point." Cade's lips flattened, so I continued explaining. "We don't really talk about the future."

"Or the present, apparently." Cade chuckled and as much as I hated to admit it, he had a point. Amy and I had been dating for years, but it had gotten to the point where we were more like friends. Neither one of us was willing to break it off, so we were just kind of waiting out the inevitable to happen.

Unfortunately, Amy becoming less of a distraction had made it hard to ignore the fact that I'd been crushing hard on Cade's little sister, Madison, for as long as I could remember. Not that I'd ever act on those feelings, for a myriad of reasons. The main one being that she probably didn't even look at me that way, anyway. She was a good girl, who studied and worked hard. She didn't need me around screwing things up for her or her family. Not to mention the fact that she was my best friend's little sister. Yeah, I doubted that would go down well.

Cade crinkled his nose. "You two are so romantic," he said sarcastically. "I can't wait to get into one of those real relationships and have sex with one girl that I hate all the time."

"I don't hate Amy."

"Then do her a favor and break up with her."

"That's a lot of hassle for something that's going to happen no matter what, anyway."

Cade shook his head. "Always the charmer. I only hope that when you get to college, you'll meet someone that you can't live without. She'll have the same interests as you, and you won't be able to stop smiling. Although, I'm not sure your face knows how to do that."

I raised my brows and blew out a breath because I *hoped* I would be different, too. Moving across the country from the one girl I couldn't get my mind off should help that.

"You coming to the gym?" Cade asked as he turned the corner in the hallway.

"Yup." I pointed my thumb over my shoulder. "I've just got to get my foam roller from my locker."

Cade's smile grew. "I bet you do."

I groaned because the team watched one viral video of a guy using his roller highly inappropriately and now these teased me, thinking *I* did all those things too. When I got to my locker, I pulled out my black foam roller, but paused because I heard some interesting noises to the side of me.

Breathy moans and loud gurgles echoed around this small section of the hallway, and I couldn't deny that my interest was piqued. I took a step to the side and the noises got louder. Really? Someone was getting lucky in the hallway? When anyone could walk past?

Horn dogs.

Curiosity got the better of me and since this was the most action I was getting for a long time, I figured I'd have a sneaky look. Quietly, I followed the sounds, trying to make my large frame less conspicuous. Turning the corner, the noises were so loud it was like I was right next to them.

Fuck.

I was.

Wait.

What.

The.

Fuck?

Amy?

Her head was tilted back, and she was smiling brightly as some random guy kissed her neck. His hand was inside her shirt and she was crying out in pleasure.

Standing there frozen, I was watching my girlfriend make out with someone else, and I didn't know what to do. So I let my reflexes take over, and threw my foam roller at the dark-haired dude coping a feel. It stunned the idiot and bounced off his head before falling to the floor and rolling to my feet.

"Da-Dash?" Amy sputtered out, looking horrified. Her cheeks were flushed and her lipstick was smeared across her face, but she didn't look unhappy about being there. I honestly didn't know what to feel, but when the guy turned around and I registered it was Henry, a teammate of mine, my pride took over.

"What the fuck are you doing, man?" I said, pushing him into the lockers, and watching as his eyes widened with horror. What the hell did he think was going to happen? They might have been under the stairs, but we were still in the hallway, and anyone could have seen them.

Henry's face was smeared with glittery lip gloss, sending a chill up my spine because I knew what it felt like to be on the receiving end of that. It was sticky and tasted like fake strawberries. I also knew that shit didn't come off for days, either.

"Dash. I'm sorry." Amy's words barely filtered through my brain as she pulled on my arm, trying to get me to distance myself from Henry. At the moment, I didn't care about her. I just needed to prove a point to my teammate.

Wait a minute. Why was I more bothered about Henry going behind my back than my girlfriend cheating on me?

Man, I really should have broken up with Amy years ago. It wasn't fair on her or me because now, she was upset for hurting me, and I couldn't care less. Really, I should have been the one that was saying sorry for even entertaining this mess.

"He-Henry?"

The hall went silent.

Or at least I thought it did because *her* voice had no problem breaking through my thoughts. Mainly because her voice played in my head like a melody even when she wasn't around.

Madison.

When I looked over at my best friend's little sister, I saw something I didn't expect. Tears. She was watching me pin Henry up against the locker and was crying about it.

Why the hell was she crying over that douche?

I looked between the two of them, and Henry's brows were furrowed.

"Madison, I can explain."

Hold on, was there something going on between them?

My fists clenched because something about that fact really pissed me off.

"Madison, is everything okay?" I asked, ready to drop Henry on the floor and take her away from this place if I had to.

She looked at me, almost embarrassed. Her lips trembled and then she dropped her gaze to the floor, taking in a deep breath.

Tiff, her cousin, was at her side in an instant and drew her into a hug.

"You're an asshole, Henry," Tiff spat out. I had no doubts that if she wasn't so busy consoling Madison, she'd slap Henry across the face because she might have been quiet, but she was feisty when she needed to be.

"I'm sorry, Madison," Henry said.

Okay, that was all the confirmation I needed. There was something going on between them.

Chuckling bitterly, I shook my head, trying to convince myself not to do something stupid.

She wasn't mine.

She never could be.

Too late.

None of my commonsense arguments worked because I'd already made my decision.

Henry had made Madison cry, so he deserved everything that was coming to him.

With Henry still pinned to the locker, I did what anyone would do in my situation. I punched him square in the face because he deserved it.

The crack of his nose echoed through the hall, and blood splattered across my face. I looked unhinged, but I didn't care. No one hurt Madison and got away with it.

"Dash, stop." Amy was clutching at my arm, doing her best to pry me away while Madison watched from my other side. She wasn't trying to stop me, so I took her lead and punched him one more time, just in case he didn't get the message with my first blow.

I was almost certain I'd broken his nose, but he could sue me and throw me in jail for all I cared. As long as I'd never have to see Madison cry again, then I'd be happy.

Shit. I probably needed to speak to someone about my obsession.

"Back up!" The principal yelled, and the crowd immediately dissipated. Madison and Amy didn't leave, though. In my haze, I almost couldn't tell them apart, they looked so much alike.

"Break it up, boys."

Principal Hader grabbed my shoulder, and he pulled me back, away from Henry. When he realized it was me, he stifled a cough.

"Daniel? What on earth are you doing?"

I wiped the blood off my face and didn't answer. Saying I was defending Madison's honor would not only confirm to everyone in the hallway that I was a simp for her, but it might freak her the fuck out.

Madison was just watching from behind the principal with awe. I hung my head in shame because I knew I shouldn't have acted like that. My mom wouldn't have liked it, but then again, she also wouldn't have liked to see a girl crying over an idiot like Henry.

"My office. Now." He pointed straight down the hallway, and the students parted like the Red Sea. I took a deep breath, ready to take my punishment because what was the worst they could do? I was graduating in two weeks. I'd passed all my classes; and had been accepted to Covey U. They could take everything they wanted away but nothing mattered more to me than making Madison feel better.

By the time Principal Hader was done lecturing me, school was out, and I was officially barred from my graduation ceremony since that was the only form of punishment he could really give me. Like I cared. It wasn't like my dad was going to be able to get the time off work, anyway. Besides, high school didn't matter nearly as much as getting a good spot in the draft next month.

Walking out of the school, it was funny knowing this would probably be the last time since I was also banned from my final classes. Again, fine by me. We were only watching movies to bypass the time, anyway.

Would I miss this place?

Nope. My best friend was coming to college with me. We'd already applied to share a dorm. I had pretty much everything I needed from this place, so maybe it was time to go.

The only thing I'd miss…well, that wasn't someone I was willing to think about much, because if I did that would be entertaining the idea that something might actually happen between us, even though I knew that wasn't possible.

"Hey, Man," Cade hollered as I walked into the parking lot. He was leaning against his old truck, waving at me. Since I had no other form of transportation, I waltzed over to him and took his hand in a bro hug.

"What are you still doing here?"

"I'm your ride, so I figured I'd wait for you. It's the least I could do after you rearranged the guy's face that upset my little sister."

"So, they were dating?"

Cade sucked in a breath and looked away. "Honestly, I'm not sure, but Tiff said Henry was an asshole and strung Madison along for a few months."

Why was I getting the urge to punch that idiot again?

"But Madison's good. She'll survive." He waved off any further questions on the topic.

"You sound awfully calm for a guy whose sister dated his teammate."

"I'm calm because the way you punched Henry's nose told every guy in this school what they needed to know. No one's going to go near her now."

"If they do, I'll happily give them the Henry Newman treatment."

"Have you spoken to Amy? I saw her eating up the drama when you left."

"Nope, and once I turn my phone on, her number's getting blocked.

"So cold, Dash, but I get it. You guys weren't exactly the example of high school sweethearts before this debacle." I cringed at the mere thought of being called a 'sweetheart,' because I didn't like people thinking I'd gone soft.

Cade tipped his chin back to the school. "How'd it go in there?"

"As expected, No more school or graduation walk."

"Ah, tough break."

"Not as tough as the break on Henry's nose."

Cade squeezed my shoulder and grinned. "Look at you trying to be funny. Honestly, I didn't think you had it in you."

"Yeah, well, sometimes you've got to laugh at the situations you end up in."

CHAPTER 3

Dash

2 Weeks Later

"Why are we here again?" I asked Cade, still making my way into the party even though I didn't want to be there.

"Because even though it's only been two weeks since I've seen you, it feels like years. A lot has happened and we need to celebrate."

"Uh, Cade. Did you forget that I saw you every day at the gym?"

"Exactly," he said as though he'd just caught me out. "The gym. Every single day. That's all you did with your forced time off. If I didn't know you better, I'd think you were some super lifelike robot that was made just to foil anyone's plans of scoring a goal."

"Okay."

He shook my shoulders, laughing. "I really thought the suspension would loosen you up, but it looks like I'm going to have to do that myself."

"We don't have time to loosen up, C. We have the draft in two weeks."

"And what are a couple of gym sessions going to do now because the teams aren't going to take into account how well you foam rolled your thighs in the last couple of weeks. On that point, Do you ever wonder if rolling your muscles that much might make you more prone to injury?"

"How the hell did you pass biology class?"

He pushed his tongue out, licking his lips. "I think we all know how I passed." He wriggled his eyebrows. No words. I had no words for my best friend because yeah, he had a thing for dangerous situations, and faculty members, apparently.

"Why did you bring me here?" I changed the subject because frankly, I didn't want to hear about him getting a blow job from our teacher. There were just certain things in our friendship that I didn't need to know. Besides, I was more suspicious about his intentions tonight because there was always a reason with Cade. He didn't do anything without an ulterior motive, and he certainly didn't drag me to parties unless he had a good reason for it.

Cade grinned. "Mandy asked me to come."

Mandy? Mandy? I tried to think about all the girls from our class, but I couldn't remember a single Mandy. However, that could just be down to me. It wasn't like I paid much attention to girls at school. There was only one that would get my attention.

"I'm surprised you're chasing her. I didn't think you wanted to be tied down with a girlfriend since we're leaving in a few weeks."

He shrugged. "I'm not planning on getting a girlfriend. It's just a little fun before we go. Something I think you'd benefit from. You might be surprised at how much you like it."

"I'm good thanks."

Cade narrowed his eyes and pointed at me. "You know. I think that's why you're a good goaltender." I responded with a glare, so he continued and pointed at my arms. "Because you're all pent up and angry. The only release you get is at the gym, and I don't think that's nearly enough for a testosterone-fueled athlete like you. But then again, sexless and angry seemed to work wonders for your save record this year. Leading the state. That's impressive." He chuckled when I didn't say anything. "Not to mention the way you messed up Henry's nose. That was insane. The guys haven't stopped talking about it. Have you seen it?"

I groaned, rolling my eyes as we walked into the house because I was frustrated that breaking a teammates nose would be my final legacy at the school. Before that, I was just the quiet goaltender that kept himself to himself. Now people saw me as something different. Something a little more unhinged. The music was blaring, and just as we got to the front door, something caught my eye. Well, more like *someone*.

"Is that Madison?" I couldn't believe what I was looking at. Madison was standing in the middle of the room dancing and waving at every guy that walked by. Tiff was next to her, watching Madison closely. I blew out breath, trying not to look like I was about to lose my shit, but I was almost certain it would happen if the guy currently talking to Madison didn't walk away. Was he the only person in the school that hadn't heard about Henry's nose?

"Ah, yeah. She's here again." Cade sighed, shaking his head in annoyance.

"Again?" That was strange. I rarely saw Madison at parties. She'd gone to one or two before, but none with this many seniors, and none where she was dressed like that. She had a tight, purple skirt on and a white cropped shirt, showing off her toned, tanned stomach.

"Yeah. In the last two weeks, my sister has decided to change things up and prove to the world that Henry's an asshole."

"How's she doing that?"

"You're looking at it." He held his hand up toward his sister and dropped it.

"And you're just going to let her walk around like that?" I glanced at her bare stomach, ignoring the tingling feeling in my fingers because I wanted to touch her so badly. "You know, I read shirts like that are bad for the kidneys?" And my health if we wanted to get specific, because I was worried I might have a heart attack just looking at her.

"Kidneys?" Cade glared at me with narrowed eyes. "You let me worry about my sister's kidneys. I'm sure they're fine, and I'm not allowed to comment on her style, anyway. My mom says I have no right. She thinks it's a phase and the more we comment on it, the more she'll do it."

"So, she's changed her style?"

"And her personality, apparently. She's been flirting with every guy that looks at her for the last two weeks."

Flirting?

With other guys.

It looked like I might have to set a few people straight before I leave.

"Is that another thing your mom told you, you had to ignore?"

Kyle, some junior, pretended to bump into Madison, and when she looked over her shoulder, he gave her an apologetic smile. I could almost hear his smarmy opening line from here. Did he seriously think he had a shot with her? Seriously. Kyle was like a second-rate kicker on the football team. No one paid him any attention, and here he was, thinking he was good enough for Madison.

"So, you're just going to let Kyle shoot his shot, then?"

"I mean, I've got a theory that if I show I care too much, she might try to date a teammate again just to provoke me."

My brows furrowed because that logic didn't make any sense.

"You don't have siblings. Trust me, it's a thing. Always trying to find new and creative ways to annoy the other one. But, anyway, if I can keep her thinking we're on the same side, then she'll be honest with me. That way, I know exactly which idiot thinks he's good enough for her, and I can speak to them before things get serious."

He gave me a pointed glare, and I had to admit, I was surprised. Cade was playing the long game, something I never expected him to do. How he could stand there and watch Kyle taking in his sister like a piece of meat, I'd never know. Especially since I was ready to push everyone out of the way and give Kyle a little makeover for it.

Madison laughed at him and touched his arm.

I winced and looked up to the ceiling. "You know what? I'm going to get some air," I said, turning and without another word, I walked out of the party with the sole intention of never walking back in. I didn't need to see that shit.

"Dash! Wait." When I heard her voice, I stopped moving. She had the ability to do that. "How the heck do you walk so fast?" She huffed out under her breath and nearly bumped into me as I turned around.

Her hands were on my chest and her eyes widened in surprise as though she wasn't just calling me. "Dash," she said with this wistful edge to it. A small smile tugged at the corners of her lips as she pushed a piece of her hair behind her ear and took me in. I couldn't help myself. I took her in too. With the purple and white outfit on, she looked like she was ready to support my new team, the Covey Crushers. Dammit. Why did she have to look so hot?

She was my teammate's sister. Only, he wasn't just a teammate. He was like a brother to me, and checking out his little sister should have been wrong, but that fact was apparently not getting through my thick skull.

I raised my hands, nearly touching her to help her gain her composure, but stopped myself, figuring her hands on my chest were enough to balance her. "Madison. What are you doing here?" I twisted my lips, stopping myself from asking why she'd left Kyle behind.

"I'm here for a good time." Her voice had this light, sweet quality to it, and I had to admit, it was nice to see her so relaxed and happy considering the last time I saw her, she looked as though her world was crumbling down.

I clenched my fists, fighting the urge to haul her over my shoulder and bring her back to my car just so I could drive her home because it wasn't my place. It also wouldn't make any sense. Hiding her away from the world wasn't fair when she was the most beautiful thing I'd ever seen, but that was exactly what I wanted to do.

Biting her bottom lip, she leaned in and poked my chest. "Plus, I kind of wanted to come because I was hoping a certain person would be here."

"Who?" I was already scanning the area for Kyle.

"You," She said so sweetly, that it took me a few seconds to register it. I looked down at her big blue eyes and damn, was that all she had to do to make my heart stop?

Shit.

I was so gone for this girl. We'd hardly spoken in the four years I'd known her, and yet, I was willing to beat up any guy who looked at her the wrong way. "I, uh," She let out a hesitant chuckle, looking to the ceiling before she mumbled. "Oh, man. This is so embarrassing."

"Spit it out, Madison."

She dragged her eyes to look at me and I could see a sense of mischief twinkling behind them.

"Everything was such a rush after the Henry debacle." Her voice was shaky but that was the only hint that she might be nervous about speaking to me. "What with you getting suspended and me having to avoid crying in

32

the hallway for an hour like some bad break up song."

"You were crying in the hallway for an hour?" My chest inflated and I immediately wanted to find Henry and break his nose all over again, but when Madison stepped toward me and rested her hand on my arm, I calmed. I couldn't help it. Something about that strawberry shampoo she used always made me feel like I was home.

"Relax. I'm fine now." She pulled me into a hug, and I wrapped one arm around her, careful to keep my hands on her back, nowhere near her butt.

As she pulled out of my hold, She kept one of her hands on my arm and let her thumb rub across my jacket. Then she let out a surprised breath before looking up at me with surprise. "Were you always this tall?" She asked with a slight grin.

"I grew six inches in the last year," I answered factually because I couldn't help but watch her reaction. Her lips were so pouty, I wondered if they felt like pillows to kiss.

When her eyes widened, I suddenly thought I'd said that last part out loud. "You're telling me, D." Pulling at my jacket, she looked me up and down again. "I don't know when this happened, but you're like a big, hulking man now."

"I am going to college in the fall, and I'm eligible to play professional hockey right now, so I guess that's a good thing."

And then there was this silence between us because that point seemed to weigh down the conversation like a heavy stone. We both knew I was leaving. With Cade. This wasn't new information, but what did feel new was the way she was looking at me. It almost felt like the same way I'd been looking at her for years, but she never noticed.

I hated myself for even thinking like this because I'd been able to push my crush to the furthest recesses of my mind all of high school, but now she was here. Looking at me like I hung the damn moon, and I was finding it hard to think about anything else other than kissing her.

Don't do it.

Don't fuckup the plan you and Cade have.

"You're welcome," I said in a lame attempt to stop thinking about her.

She tilted her head, confused. Did she forget why she came over to speak to me in the first place?

"For breaking Henry's nose. The guy had it coming. I only wish I' been able to punch him in the gut a couple of times before I got caught."

"Honestly, it was the most romantic thing anyone has ever done for me."

Slack-jawed, I stared at her awestruck face. Did she just say romantic? Did she know how I felt or was she having love-struck ideations after everything that happened? It had to be the latter. I was the only one thinking things I shouldn't.

"If that's the most romantic thing to have ever happened to you, then you're looking at the wrong kind of guys."

She squared her shoulders, pressing her lips together. Somehow, I'd managed to piss her off. "What do you mean? Why wouldn't I want a guy that would defend me and make me feel like I was special?"

Fuck. Fuck. Fuck.

This conversation was skating a dangerous territory. A territory I knew I needed to get out of immediately.

"Have you seen Cade?"

Her hand finally dropped from my chest, along with her gaze falling to the floor. She couldn't look at me, and I guessed it was because what I said felt a lot like rejection. It wasn't. I was just given nowhere else to go.

"He's inside, but I think he went up to a room with some girl. It's probably something you don't want to interrupt and it's definitely something I don't want to see."

"Okay," I replied curtly, looking over her head and back into the party. I couldn't exactly leave after asking that question but going back in there felt like torture. "I guess I'll see you later."

"Sure."

Without another word, I walked past Madison and shook my head. She wasn't flirting with me. That was just all in my head. I was just too far gone for her to think straight anymore. At least, that was what I let myself believe.

I took a step toward the door, but I couldn't leave. Not after that. I needed to watch Madison, and make sure she was okay, especially if her brother was busy.

CHAPTER 4

Madison

"Are you still watching him?" Tiff leaned in to ask as I stared down the grumpy goalie that had been the chief topic of interest for me in the last two weeks.

"He's just standing by the drinks on his own. I thought he was leaving, but he stayed, so maybe I should go and talk to him."

"No. Don't do that."

"But isn't standing by the drinks a universal sign that you want to strike up a conversation with someone?"

"No, it's not."

I turned to look at my cousin with a raised brow. "Mhm. Are you sure because I believe I saw you talking with a hot, private school kid at that party we went to last week."

The mere mention of him made her clamp her lips shut. Her cheeks got a little red and she tipped her chin down, suddenly getting shy on me. That was new for my quippy cousin.

I gasped, turning my body so I could completely focus on her.

"Wait a minute. Did something happen?"

She looked around as though someone might care about our conversation. They wouldn't. We'd just gate crashed a graduation party, so no one cared about a couple of sophomores gossiping in the corner.

"Tiffany Anne Bright. You're going to tell me what happened right now, or I'm going to go through your phone history and find out myself."

She pushed out an annoyed breath. "You won't find anything in there. He hasn't texted me since."

"Since?" My mouth dropped and I needed information right now. "What happened and why haven't you told me?"

"I didn't want to talk about it."

"But now you do? At a party."

"You were the one that brought him up. I thought you'd forgotten about him."

"How could I forget? It's the first guy you've shown any remote interest in. So tell me more."

She bit back a smile before saying, "He was really cute, and really nice. I thought we had a connection."

I smiled. "Aw, so you like him?"

"What's there not to like? He was sweet, funny and-"

My eyes widened and I could barely breathe. "Tiff. Do you want him to be your boyfriend?" it was a question I didn't think I'd be asking until college, but I was going with it.

She shook her head, and her smile fell a little. "Even if I did, it's not going to happen. He, uh, gave me a wrong number."

"What? Are you serious?"

"Yeah." She waved it off, but it was obvious she was still upset by it. "It's not a big deal. These things happen all the time."

"Not to you. You're amazing and any guy that doesn't see that, doesn't deserve you."

"Maybe you're right. It's just, well, I just really liked him. Like really liked him."

Her cheeks blushed, and then it hit me like a hard stone.

"Tiff," I said with an uneasy edge. "How far did you go with him? "

Her lips curved into an almost embarrassed smile. "We might have done a little more than kissing."

Shit. More than kissing?

"How much more?"

She bit her bottom lip, and there was my answer.

"Tiff, did you have sex with him?"

"Uh."

"At a party?!"

She shook her head. "I had a drink which loosened me up and one thing sort of led to another."

My jaw dropped, and I closed my eyes, shaking my head in disbelief because this wasn't Tiff. "I feel like I've been thrown into another dimension because this couldn't be happening. You. Tiff Bridges. Had sex with a random guy at a party."

"He wasn't a random guy. I liked him a lot and I really thought there was just something there. We just kind of clicked."

"You clicked so much that you just opened your legs? After all the shit you've been giving me about Henry?" She pursed her lips together and didn't answer. Probably because she finally realized how shitty that was. "I can't believe it. You haven't even had a boyfriend, and yet you slept with some random guy at a party?"

My brows crossed, and I studied her because I really didn't get it. I couldn't figure it out. This wasn't Tiff, and it certainly wasn't like Tiff to wait to tell me about it, either.

She closed her eyes, cringing at the thought. "I know. I know now it was a stupid mistake, but you didn't see his eyes close up. They were this pearly green color, and he had this laugh that made my heart flutter. Then, when he kissed me, I felt all these raw emotions, and I guess one thing led to another, and it just, kind of happened."

"You can say that again," I muttered, trying not to be annoyed at my cousin. This was a big moment for her, but I didn't feel excited for her. Just last month, she was berating me for thinking about having sex with Henry and I was with him for six months. She was with this dude for six minutes and thought it was a good idea to give up her goodies.

I shook my head in disbelief. "When did that even happen? I was with you the entire night."

Tiff pushed her lips from side to side "I think it was when you were playing beer pong with that couple. What were their names? Mike and Olivia?"

"I have no idea what their names were. I was just enjoying the party. So were you, apparently." I crossed my arms, keeping my focus on the people dancing in front of me. Something about this didn't feel right, and I didn't know what it was.

Tiff elbowed me in the rib. "Come on, don't be like that."

"Like what?"

"Pissed off. I know I should have said something sooner, but I didn't know how to bring it up after everything that happened with you and Henry."

"It's easy. You just say, 'hey Mads. You remember that party where I was talking to the cute guy with the slightly wide-set jaw? well, I bonked him in the bathroom when you weren't paying attention.'"

Tiff was taken aback and blew out a humorless breath. "Honestly, I don't think I could have said it quite as eloquently as you."

I tried to hold back my smile because I wanted to be a little annoyed with her, but I wasn't. Ultimately, Tiff's hesitance had meant I hadn't made the worst decision of my life in actually sleeping with Henry. Tiff acted on a whim and berating her for a choice she'd already made wasn't going to make the situation better.

"How was it?" I asked, taking a sip of my drink and scanning the party, pretending I wasn't looking at Dash. Still at the drinks station and hot as ever.

"It was good. I think."

I raised a brow, looking at my cousin in amusement. "You think? You know, I'm obviously not an expert but if you have to think about it, I'm guessing it wasn't that great."

"Is the first time supposed to be good, though?"

"I'll let you know when I've experienced it." Reluctantly, I looked back at the crowd, feeling a little depressed about the predicament I found myself in. I couldn't pinpoint why I was feeling this way, though. It wasn't that I was jealous of Tiff for having sex, but something about it was throwing me off. Maybe it was because I'd been so open to talking to her about having sex with Henry before and she just went and did it like it wasn't a big deal.

"Don't worry. It's not like it's going to happen again," Tiff muttered. My shoulders slumped in sadness for my friend. She wasn't the type of girl to go after guys, so she must have really liked him.

"Who knows, it's only been a week, he might still call you back."

"I didn't get the opportunity to give him my number."

"What?"

"He apparently didn't have his phone on him. I'm also ninety-nine percent certain he gave me a fake name because when I looked up Thatcher Hastings, it definitely wasn't the guy I was talking to."

"Tiff, that sucks." I rested my hand on her arm and rubbed my thumb across the fabric of her shirt. She just stared at the floor.

"Who wants to play Spin the Bottle?" Sidney Wiliams yelled across the room, holding an empty vodka bottle in her hand, and parading around like it was a trophy. A few people followed her, sitting in the middle of the room to create a circle.

When she saw Dash standing by the drinks, desperate and brooding, she sauntered over to him and said something that convinced him to move. Albeit, slowly and still somewhat reluctantly.

My heart spiked, and I stood, immediately spurring into action.

"What are you doing?" Tiff asked, making no effort to move herself.

"I'm going to play a little game." What I couldn't admit to her was that hearing that she lost her virginity had suddenly made me feel like I needed to make a little more progress myself.

I was naïve with Henry, but not in love. No. I realized that the minute I saw Dash look at me when he punched Henry. *That* was love. That was what I was craving. A wild depravity that only Dash knew how to deliver.

Other students made room for Dash's bulky frame in the circle, and I nearly laughed watching him attempt to sit cross-legged in such a tiny space.

"Madison. Are you joining us?" Sidney asked, patting the spot right next to her.

I couldn't help myself. I looked at Dash and saw the confusion across his face. Standing straight, I smiled smugly. "Yes. I'm ready," I hummed out and dropped to the floor, careful to sit so my underwear wasn't showing.

I looked around the circle, surprised I didn't really know anyone but Dash, Kyle, Jessa and Sidney. The rest were just random juniors and seniors that I'd never spoken to. I should have been intimidated, but I wasn't. Being constantly dragged to Cade's games meant that I was used to hanging out with people older than me, and I was pretty comfortable with that.

Sidney gently placed the bottle in the middle of the circle and assessed the people around it.

"Alright, shall we let Kyle start?" She said with a flirty edge. I couldn't help but notice she gave him a little wink when she leaned back.

Kyle didn't seem to notice or care, he just spun the bottle and waited for it to slow. When it landed on Hayley, the smallest of smiles graced his lips. One of his friends ribbed him and he bent forward, cupping her face before kissing her fully. I swallowed down the feeling in my stomach. Was that how you were supposed to kiss? With all that tongue and spit? Even in front of all these people, there was passion. Way more than I'd ever experienced with Henry.

Crap. Why did I suddenly feel really inadequate? If that bottle landed on me, and I had to kiss one of these people, were they going to laugh at how bad I was because of my lack of experience?

Round and round the bottle spun, but for some reason, it never stopped on me. Maybe karma was playing a trick on me? Maybe I was never supposed to have a guy interested in me? Or maybe it was a cosmic force helping me because they didn't want me embarrassing myself.

When Jessa spun the bottle and it landed on Dash, my heart nearly fell to the floor. Dash was about to kiss another girl in front of me and I had to smile about it because we weren't dating. Not that there was ever a chance for that, but I wished I'd assessed the situation before sitting down.

Dash looked around the circle, and his eyes slowed when they got to me. I masked my hurt with a grin that could rival any beauty pageant. I was going to be happy. This was a new Madison. I would never cry over another boy, especially one that had no idea I was crushing on him.

Dash looked at Jessa, and if he was trying to be subtle, it wasn't working. His frown was evident from here, but since that seemed to be a staple for his face, Jessa wasn't put off by it. She just got on her hands and knees and crawled over to him. I thought she was trying to be sexy, but with the upbeat music in the background, it just looked weird.

"Are you ready for me?" She purred.

I wanted to vomit. This wasn't something I needed to see.

Dash leaned back the closer she got, and it wasn't until his back was against the sofa that he gave into her kissing him. His eyes widened when she rested her hand on his cheek, and she dipped her chin, looking to deepen the kiss. Dash batted her off pretty quickly, which was the only saving grace of the night. Imagine if he'd have liked it, and I had to watch that.

A shiver ran up my spine because this little crush I'd suddenly developed on Dash was getting out of hand. He'd been around me for years and I'd always thought he was cute, but I never thought about him like this. Now, I couldn't stop.

His smile. His eyes. His constantly furrowed brow. It all did it for me.

I wanted him so badly it hurt.

"It's your turn, Dash," some girl said, and I couldn't help but notice Dash's gaze flick to me again for a nano second. There was an emotion behind his eyes that I couldn't decipher because he looked away too quickly. I wanted to say it was shame, but that could have been me projecting, desperately hoping he liked me the way I liked him even after he brushed me off earlier.

Dash spun the bottle with little enthusiasm, and I watched it with more eagerness than a child waiting to open their first present on Christmas day.

Please be me. Please be me. Please be me.

I really hoped I wasn't thinking that so loudly that people could hear it. My eyes didn't stop watching the glass bottle because I desperately wanted to kiss Dash and convince him that we were meant for each other. A childish dream, some might say, but I felt something, I just didn't know how to describe it. If only he'd take the first step. Then, maybe we'd have a chance.

When the bottle stopped directly between Sydney and me, I couldn't speak. Had I nearly manifested my wants into existence?

"It's split," Kyle stated the obvious. "What are we supposed to do now?"

"Well," Sydney drawled out. "It means the person who spun the bottle gets to decide who he wants to kiss. Me or Madison." She pointed at me with a little distaste in her voice, but I ignored it. Mainly because I couldn't move. Too worried that I might pee myself with excitement. Was Tiff watching this? I could only hope she had her phone out so she could record my first kiss with Dash, and we could replay this at our wedding in years to come.

Dash looked between the two of us, and then at something over my shoulder. Again, I was too invested in Dash's decision to look away from him. If he picked me, I'd get to kiss him.

Kissing Dash.

My brain was short-circuiting, thinking over all the possibilities.

"Come on, Dash. We don't have all night."

He was still looking between us and when he sighed and leaned over, something in my gut was telling me that he was going to choose me. I wasn't sure I was ready, but would I ever be ready for my first kiss with Dash? Probably not, but I needed this. We both did.

He crept a little closer and I'd officially stopped breathing now. I closed my eyes in preparation, and when I felt his presence, I tried not to squeal, even though I could feel myself sweating.

The room started cheering, and I opened my eyes.

Shattered.

What was left of my heart was shattered to pieces on the floor. Dash kissed Sydney. Granted, it must have been quick because it was over before I'd even opened my eyes. The only reason I knew it happened was because Dash was already back in his seat, grumbling something to himself.

"Madison." My brother's voice from behind startled me, and when I looked over my shoulder to see him glaring at me, I didn't know what to do. "I think you're done for the night."

Well, that was enough to completely ruin the mood. Not that there was one because without even trying Dash broke my heart. He used the blade from his hockey boot and scratched it up until it was sliced into pieces.

I'd put myself out there so many times tonight, but maybe it was time to finally accept the L. Dash didn't want me, it was obvious now. He chose Sydney, and if he was acting like it was a chore to kiss her, imagine how bad he'd be if he'd kissed me. I guessed having two guys clearly thinking kissing me was unpleasant in less than a month would ruin my reputation. So, maybe that was Dash's way of doing me a favor.

"You know what?" I squeaked out, pulling myself up as gracefully as I could. "I think you're right. I need to go."

"Aw man," Kyle said, which I ignored. He was cute, but he wasn't Dash. The guy that would do anything to protect me, except date me, of course.

"Come on, Tiff." Tiff, who was standing by Cade, sprung into action, and followed behind me. I didn't look back. What was the point? I assumed everyone was laughing at me anyway.

"How are we getting home?" Tiff asked as we walked out of the front door, making me slow. She had a good point. I'd been drinking, and I was supposed to be driving.

"Well, crap. We're going to have to wait for Cade or get an Uber."

"I'll drive you." I flicked my surprised gaze to Dash. What was he doing out here?

"You don't have to," I said with the sweetest smile, trying to pretend that his earlier rejection meant nothing, because it wasn't his fault I'd built up this entire thing in my head.

"Well, I'm not letting you drive. I can smell the alcohol on your breath from here."

"What about Cade?"

"What about him? He's a big boy, he can take care of himself. Besides, I think he occupied himself after you left."

Dash didn't say anything else, he just pushed past me, and I assumed started walking to his car.

Tiff gave me a pointed look, but in the dark, I couldn't really tell if she was angry or happy about the situation. "At least he has heated seats," She whispered, dutifully following behind Dash. Okay, I guessed she was happy then. Maybe she didn't see my humiliation in there, or maybe a nice, toasty butt on the ride home was more important. I took my time following them and when we got to the car, I stood behind Tiff, who was about to get into the back seat.

When she saw me, she scowled. "What are you doing?"

"Getting in the car with you." I pointed to the door, confused.

"Are you kidding me? Get in the front. I left the front for you."

"Why?"

"Because after that performance in there, you both clearly need to talk."

"What do you mean?"

She rolled her eyes and pushed me away. "Just get in the car," she hissed before slamming the door in my face.

Well, okay then.

I sighed and opened the front car door, giving Dash a little wave as I did. "Hey, Big Man. Long time, no see." I smiled, but as per usual, Dash didn't return it.

As I slid onto the leather seat and buckled my seat belt, I paused when I realized Dash was still looking at me. "What?"

"Big Man?"

"It's your new nickname because you're this Big Man now." I flittered my hand in front of his face. Seriously, it had been what? Two weeks since I last saw him, and I don't know what happened, but he had suddenly turned into this rugged, sexy guy. Okay, maybe it wasn't the elapse of time that did it. Maybe it was the fact that I started seeing him differently after he punched Henry. He wasn't just my grumbly brother's best friend anymore. He was my protector, now, and something about that made him hugely appealing.

Dash rolled his eyes at my antics, and as per usual, grumbled something under his breath. I glanced over my shoulder to the backseat, making eye contact with Tiff who just shook her head. I had no idea why. I was just being my usual self. Or should I say, my *new* usual self because I refused to let any guy make me feel vulnerable again. They just weren't worth it.

The ride to Tiff's house was quiet, but Dash filled the void with a playlist that I could only describe as angsty and depressing. It was the type of music that the front man slurred his words so much; it sounded more like groaning than anything else. I guessed that was why Dash liked it.

After dropping Tiff off, he turned the music down, which was surprising. What wasn't surprising was that Dash didn't talk. So, I decided to fill the void and talked all about the gossip he missed out on over the last two weeks. There wasn't much, and he didn't seem that interested, but I preferred that to sitting in an awkward silence.

As he stopped outside my house, I turned to him with a smile. "Thanks for the ride home, Big Man. You saved me at least twenty bucks on an Uber."

"No problem." He still wasn't looking at me, which made it hard to know what to do next. "I'm, uh, just going to head inside now." I pointed with my thumb out the window to my house. A couple of the lights were on, and I suspected my parents were still up, waiting for me and Cade.

He mumbled something under his breath, which I assumed was 'okay'.

Leaning over, I opened the car door, but stopped when I thought I heard Dash say something.

"What was that?" I relaxed back into the seat, looking at him.

He cleared his throat. "I said you deserve better." It was still a mumble, but I understood it this time.

"You deserve better than being kissed by a bunch of drunk idiots in the middle of some random house while you play a lackluster game of Spin The Bottle."

"Um. Okay. Thanks."

Where the hell did that come from?

Was this his way of trying to make me feel better about how he'd rather kiss anyone but me.

When he didn't say anything else, I assumed that was it, so I opened the door. "I'll see you later, Big Man."

"You deserve to be with a guy that will make you their everything." With my legs perched over the edge of the seat, I sat quietly for a minute and stared out into the darkness toward my house. "The guys you're going after are only showing you an ounce of what you deserve. You don't need to change the way you dress or act to get attention. You've already got it without trying."

When I slowly turned to look at him, Dash was watching me intently.

"Make them work for it and only do things you want to do. Don't come to parties just because you want to prove you're over some idiot that wasn't worth your time in the first place."

I silently nodded. It was the first time in my life that I was rendered speechless because I'd never heard Dash speak so passionately about something before, and that something was me.

What the heck is going on?

"Thanks," I finally mumbled, not sure what else to do. He didn't say anything else, but his fingers gripped the steering wheel so tightly that his knuckles were going white. "I, uh, guess I'll see you around."

I moved out of the car, shutting the door, and shuffling up to my house without looking back because I had no idea what just happened between us, but the fluttering feeling in my stomach was making me believe something else might be starting between us.

CHAPTER 5

Dash

Two Months Later

"The Atlanta Anglerfish choose Cade Bright, defenseman, as the tenth pick of the first-round."

Cade smiled and waved at the camera as he stood. The crowd cheered as he hugged his parents and sister before giving me a high-five. "It's you next, D. I can feel it." He grinned, talking just loud enough that I could hear it over the noise in the stadium. There was no time to say congratulations because Cade was already walking down the stairs to the table filled with cameras and his new manager.

First round.

I couldn't believe it. I fully expected Cade to get picked high, he was a great defenseman, after all, but in the first round as the tenth pick. Well, that was incredible.

Clapping, I smiled as I watched my best friend's dreams come true. The same dreams we'd been talking about for nearly eight years now. I wondered what it would feel like to get drafted. To know that you had your future planned out and where you were going to live after you graduated college. It was all things I wanted, but as the night continued, I was getting nervous that it might not happen for me.

As the excitement died down, I took my seat, along with the rest of Cade's family. As expected, his mother was crying, and his dad was watching on proudly as Cade was busy on the stage taking photos with his new jersey.

My knees were shaking, so I ran a hand through my hair, then looked at the stage again. I was nervous as hell, and the empty seat next to me wasn't helping my mood.

"Dash, Honey?" Cade's mom leaned over so that I could see her. "Do you think your dad will be able to make it?"

"I, uh, doubt it," I eased out, giving her the best smile I could muster. "There was an emergency at the firehouse. He said he'll try but I doubt they'll let him in."

She pressed her lips together, forcing out a sad smile. "I'm sorry, sweetie. I'll make sure to record every second, so he'll feel like he was here."

"Appreciate it." I stopped short of saying anything else because I didn't want to get myself worked up. For someone who prided themselves in being calm, I was feeling a lot of things tonight, but none of them were excitement.

What if I didn't get drafted at all? What would I do? I hadn't built a plan up other than becoming an NHL goaltender and that fact was starting to make me nervous.

"Excuse me." A woman dressed in black with a microphone smiled at our row. "Are you Cade Bright's parents?" When they nodded, she asked, "Would you mind coming down to the stage with me for a few minutes? We'd love to ask you some questions, and also take a few pictures with

Cade."

"Of course. Can my daughter come too?" Cade's mom asked, pointing to Madison.

Madison raised her hand. "Don't worry. I'm fine here. I don't want Dash to be lonely."

Why the hell did she have to say shit like that and expect me to be fine with it?

Something passe between the Brights, and it was then I realized, she was staying behind because she pitied me. She didn't want me sitting here on my own while I watched everyone else get picked around me, and although that was a sweet gesture, it made me feel pathetic.

"If you're sure, Mads?" Her dad squeezed her knee, checking on final time.

"Yeah, I'm sure. Dash is going to get picked next, anyway. Want to make sure I witness it."

"Good luck, D," Cade's dad said before they followed the camera crew.

I leaned back in my chair and rested my hands on my knees, not sure what to do with myself. Madison and I were alone. Something that I made sure wouldn't happen after I got very close to admitting how much she meant to me. It was a stupid move, one that I would regret forever because I gave her something that felt a lot like hope. Hope that maybe something could happen between us. It couldn't. I'd solidified that decision in the last two months by avoiding her as much as possible.

"You good, Big Man?" Madison asked, and I grumped out a response because anything else risked sounding like a declaration of love.

I took a sharp breath, taking my time to blow it out as I watched Cade getting his picture taken while his parents proudly watched on. We had at least another five minutes before the next pick was due and I had no idea what to talk about with Madison.

Madison crossed her legs, bringing her heeled toe into my view, and I couldn't help myself. I followed the line of her shoe all the way up her smooth legs to the hem of her skirt.

Stop looking.

My brain was telling me things I didn't want to hear. It was only when I realized she was discreetly texting someone that the voice drowned out.

Who was she messaging?

I straightened my back, hoping I could get a glance at her screen, but her perfectly curled hair was blocking my view.

"Who are you texting?" I asked, so intrigued that I couldn't stop myself.

She jumped when she heard my voice and quickly turned her phone off and stuffed it into her purse before I could see anything. Flicking her hair over her shoulder, she gave me a forced, sweet smile. I knew what that meant.

She was texting a guy.

Suddenly, my stomach hurt, but I put it down to the lack of food in this place, not the fact that Madison had already moved on. I might have told her that she deserved someone better in the car after that stupid party, but I didn't expect her to go out and find another one so quickly.

I wasn't surprised, though. Madison was hot. So hot that sometimes I forgot to breathe around her.

"No one."

I raised a brow. "You sure? Because I've never heard you snort so loud at Tiff."

Throwing her chin up, she rested her head against the theater-style seat and groaned.

"I don't think it's any of your business who I'm messaging."

I growled, adjusting my jacket before slumping in my seat. "Maybe not, but it would be great to know as distraction." I gestured to everything that was going on below. Cade was now taking pictures with his parents and it looked as though discussions with the teams over the next pick were underway.

"Fine," Madison sighed dramatically. "If you must know, it's Kyle. There. I said it. Go ahead and tell me that I deserve someone better. That I need someone who won't stop thinking about me, or whatever you said last time." She huffed out an annoyed breath. "But, honestly? It feels like I'm going to be waiting for eighty-seven years if I don't start putting some work in."

"That's a little dramatic. You waited two weeks." I was trying to hide my annoyance because it felt like she hadn't heard me in the car. She was worth more than any of the guys in our town could give her. If she wasn't going to willingly take that advice, then I was just going to have to force it on her, by speaking to every single guy I could.

"That's like two years in teen years, don't you know."

"You are something else." I shook my head, hoping she couldn't see just how pissed off I was. "But I can't believe out of all the people at North Central High, you'd pick Kyle." My lip curled as I said his name, and I was thinking about all the ways I could discreetly text him before the end of the night.

"Why not? Just because you didn't want to kiss me during Spin the Bottle, doesn't mean that everyone in the circle felt the same way." Her voice was so smug that I wanted to tell her I saw him sneaking into a room with Hayley at a different party last week, but I didn't. After seeing how crushed she was about Henry, I vowed to never see her like that again. So, I'd just have to make sure Kyle ended it before it got that far.

"That's not what happened," I muttered, knowing she wouldn't be able to hear me over all the noise in the room. What she didn't realize was that the only reason Sidney pulled me into the game was because she said she was going to invite Madison for me. If I didn't go, then she'd be kissing someone else and there was no chance of that happening. I fully intended on picking her when the bottle landed in between her and Sidney, but I couldn't. Her brother was standing on the opposite side of the room, watching me like a hawk, serving as a constant reminder that she wasn't mine, and she never would be. She was Cade's *little* sister, and I was going to college. We weren't meant to be together, and maybe the distance would do me some good.

"Can everyone please take their seats, the next draft pick is about to be announced."

Madison squealed and when the lights went down, she leaned over and asked, "Which team is picking next?"

"The Anglerfish again. They got this spot through a trade last year." She grinned and I hated that I knew exactly what she was thinking. It wasn't going to happen. There was no way in hell that I was going to get picked straight after Cade, and to the same team. It just wasn't possible.

"Good luck, Big Man."

"Thanks," I mumbled. My leg was shaking, and I pushed my palm down, trying to stop it. When that didn't work, I took a few deep breaths and closed my eyes. Nope. My heel was still tapping the floor. Nothing was going to calm me in this situation.

Nothing until Madison rested her palm on top of my hand. Then, suddenly, my foot stopped. She laced her fingers with mine and I felt my heart slow, and it was as if we were the only two people in this stadium.

Without realizing, I squeezed her hand.

"You don't need to be nervous. You're going to get picked any second now. I can feel it."

I felt something too, but it wasn't the same thing as her. Deep in my chest, I felt a yearning need to be close to her. With her hand in mine, my heart suddenly thought it might be able even be possible.

"Madison, I-"

When she looked at me, I paused, completely forgetting what I was going to say.

"For the eleventh pick of the first round, the Atlanta Anglerfish have selected Daniel Bridges, Goaltender."

My brows crossed, because, had I just heard that correctly? Had they just said my name?

Judging by the tight squeeze of Madison's hand and the camera crew waiting at the end of the row, I'd say yes.

I don't know what possessed me to stand, but I figured Madison must have pulled me up, realizing that I wasn't going to move myself. She threw her arms around me, giving me a tight hug while I stood there, feeling slightly delirious.

"I knew it," she sang into my ear while she patted me on the back. "You were always destined for greatness, and I'm so proud of you."

"Thank you for being here." It was all I managed to say before the camera crew ushered me to the front of the room. As I stepped out of my row, I quickly kissed my fingers and pointed to the sky, thanking my mother in heaven before I took those daunting steps toward my future.

CHAPTER 6

Madison

I clapped as I watched Dash walk down the stairs.

They did it.

Tears were threatening to fall because, somehow, my brother and his best friend managed to make it to the same NHL team. The dream they had talked about since they were ten years old was somehow coming true, and I couldn't believe it but the happiness I felt for them burned inside me like a roaring fire.

Still standing and clapping like a performing seal, I realized I was now amongst in an empty row of chairs with no one to smile or talk to. Right. Well, I better sit.

Blowing out a breath, I relaxed into my seat, wondering when my parents would be back, or Cade for that matter. They were no longer on the stage, so I hoped they'd come back soon, and weren't planning on leaving me here for the rest of the night.

Dash shook his new manager's hand, and the pit of my stomach simmered with something other than hunger. Dash was...well, he was always handsome, but I'd never seen him in a suit before, and he looked good. Better than good. The suit fit him in all the right places, emphasizing just how tall and muscular he was. If I wasn't already hot for Dash, then I'd be feral over him now.

But alas, after that Spin the Bottle debacle, I was almost certain Dash wasn't interested in me. At least, that was what I continually said to myself. It was just, there were a couple of things that made me second guess myself. The way he looked at me just before his name was announced being one of them, the things he said to me in the car when he drove me home, the fact that he'd been avoiding me since the incident. Things weren't adding up.

I felt my phone buzz in my pocket, and I immediately took it out, expecting to see something from Kyle. Admittedly, I wasn't that interested in him, but when he messaged me after Spin the Bottle, telling me he wished I stayed, I didn't feel like there was any harm talking to him. It was also helping fix my now fragile ego after Henry so casually tossed me aside.

When the phone lit up, I frowned when I saw the message.

Tiff: SOS

Not the type of message I was expecting considering she knew where I was.

Madison: There's not enough signal for a call here. What's wrong?

Tiff: Something that I really don't want to share via text. Can I come to yours tonight? I desperately need help.

Madison: Of course! You know where the key is. Not sure how long we'll be there, but I'll message you when I'm on my way back.

58

Tiff is typing…

As I waited for her response, someone cleared their throat and when I looked up, it was the same woman that had spoken to my parents before.

"I'm sorry to bother you, ma'am, but are you Daniel Bridges's sister?"

"Uh." My mouth was hanging open like a fish as I looked between the lady and the camera crew filming behind her. "I'm a friend." I left it at that.

"Oh, you're his girlfriend," She said, turning to the camera crew. "Can we ask you a couple of questions?"

"Oh, um."

Before I could really deny anything, the woman had managed to usher me out of the row.

"Nothing too intense. Just a few fluffy questions about Daniel that we can put out with our online marketing."

"Uhm." Should I correct her? Looking between her and the camera crew, I realized if I didn't answer these questions, then no one else would. Dash wouldn't have something to look back on and who was I to deny him that privilege?

"Follow me." She started walking down the steps toward the stage and I guessed I had no choice but to follow her. Watching my heels, I made my way down the steps, not sure what I was doing, but in too deep to stop.

As the heat of the lights hit my skin, Dash made eye contact with me.

"Madison? What are you doing here?"

"Smile, Big Man," I said, mine never faltering as I extended my arms and pulled him into a hug.

"What's going on?" He whispered in my ear and although we were on a stage with thousands of people watching us, it felt like this was the closest thing to a quiet moment we'd have.

"I just wanted you to know you had someone rooting for you here."

Pulling away, his eyes bore into mine, and looked at me the same way he did earlier. I felt something deep in my bones. Something I wasn't sure I'd ever feel again. His lips parted slightly, and I was on the tips of my toes, waiting for him to finish off what he was saying before his name was announced, but then he quickly shut his mouth.

Nothing. He was going to say nothing again, and I couldn't help but be disappointed, because it felt like he was holding something back and I desperately wanted to know what it was.

What was on his mind? I was more than happy to tell him what was on mine.

"Congratulations, Big Man," I said before I was ushered to the side as he took pictures with his new manager and team jersey. Oh, how I wanted to steal it and sleep in it every night. Too bad that was only in my head because after this, Dash was leaving. He'd go to college and be some hot shot goalie and forget about me.

"I'm sorry. We didn't get your name earlier." The woman asked. I glanced down at the microphone now sitting by my chin and realized that I was going to have to speak. The camera was live and I didn't want to embarrass Dash, so I decided to go with it and have a little fun. It was just a few fluffy questions, after all. How bad could they be?

"I'm Madison."

"Great. So, Madison, how do you feel about Daniel getting drafted in the first round?"

"I'm so excited for him. Das-Daniel is one of the most loyal and determined guys I've ever met. He deserves this and every other success that comes his way."

Dash's words from the beginning of summer suddenly echoed through my head again. *"You deserve a guy that will make you their everything."* Was he going to say something like that again tonight after finding out about Kyle? It felt like it, but what did I know? I had one boyfriend who was obviously cheating on me, but I was too infatuated to notice.

"His dad couldn't make it tonight, unfortunately, but I know he'd want me to say how proud he was, too."

"And going to do anything tonight to celebrate?"

Kiss him. I smiled before taming my lips into a frown because I didn't want the camera giving my thoughts away. No. Kissing him was only something I thought about it my dreams lately. No wonder Cade was worried about me getting up so late. I wasn't sleeping well, I could admit that, but it wasn't just down to Henry as Cade thought. It was down to a lot of things.

Huge changes were about to happen in my life. My brother was moving across the country, and he was taking his best friend with him. A fact that I would have been fine with three short months ago. But now, I wasn't so sure.

"Dash is pretty low key, so we'll probably just celebrate with a quiet night in."

Why was I having visions of me and Dash sitting on my sofa, eating popcorn while he grumbled about the romcom I was forcing him watch?

Had I become obsessed with Dash?

I wasn't sure, but the more I stood there and talked about him, the more I wanted to text Kyle and tell him I was taken because my heart wouldn't be owned by anyone else at this point.

"You must be very proud."

"I am."

The wide smile instantly dropped. "Thank you so much." And that was all she said before she walked away.

Dash's girlfriend? My heart fluttered at the mere thought even though my brain knew I was being delusional.

But was delusion really that bad?

CHAPTER 7

Dash

Madison was standing in front of me, talking to the reporter and I could hear every single word.

She was proud of me? Did she really say that? Why did those unprompted words make me want to stand a little straighter?

I shook my head, cursing out because I knew it was wrong. So. Damn. Wrong.

Saddling up next to her, she jumped a little when she realized I was there. "Dash," she said in this breathy, kind of hot way.

I thanked the reporter and when she was far enough away, I leaned into Madison.

"Have you been telling people you're my girlfriend?"

She blushed at my words, and shit, it was the cutest thing I'd ever seen. I kept my mouth in a tight line, stopping myself from smiling because I liked it.

Pointing to the camera crew, she said, "Yeah, sorry about that. They came over asking for your family, and I didn't want them thinking you had no one here." She tucked a piece of hair behind her ear and looked to the floor. "I also kind of wanted to be on TV too," She said in what felt like an after thought.

"What's Kyle going to think when he sees it?"

Yeah, I wasn't through mentioning that idiot because I was butt hurt about the entire situation, but I was okay with it. Mainly because in between talking to my new manager and Madison, I'd already sent him a message, warning him to back off.

She waved a hand in front of me. "Ah, Kyle won't mind. He's nothing serious. Just a little someone to get my mind off my loneliness."

A low growl emanated from my chest, but thankfully, the noise in the stadium was so loud, there was no way she could hear it.

Get her mind off her loneliness?

Fuck me.

She was trying to kill me.

"Nice jersey you got there." She brought her hand forward to lift my new jersey before letting it fall. "You're officially an Atlanta Anglerfish now."

"Technically, I have another three years until that's going to happen. "

Her nose crinkled and she looked around the room. "Wait, are you telling me your place on the team isn't guaranteed?"

"Technically, it's a contract to state that they have first dibs on me after they think I've developed enough."

She looked me up and down and let out a snort. "I think you've developed just fine."

My fingers gripped my jersey tighter, and I held back from saying anything, but I wasn't sure how I felt about this new 'flirty' Madison. It was like she suddenly had no filter, and I wondered if she was talking to other guys like that too.

"Thank you."

"For?" She raised a brow in question.

I pointed at the camera crew "For doing that for me. I appreciate it."

Her smile grew and she slapped me on the shoulder. "Anything for you, Big Man."

Her eyes connected with mine, and I did something completely unexpected. I hauled her into my arms, and squeezed her tightly to show just how much I appreciated her.

"Geez, Dash, are you trying to break my back, or something?" She joked, patting me on the back.

Coming out of the tight hold, I didn't let her get very far. Still close enough that our breath was mingling, I wanted to kiss her. To do what I should have done at that stupid party, and let her know just how beautiful and perfect I thought she was.

But as her eyes flicked between my lips and eyes, I knew I couldn't.

She was my best friend's little sister, and not only had I not talked to her brother about this crush, but I was leaving. Covey U was only a few weeks away and what was I going to do? Have a long distance relationship with Madison?

No. I couldn't. She deserved better than that. Better than me. Better than anyone here.

"Dash." Cades voice broke through the tension and I immediately stepped back, looking at my best friend. "We did it, bro."

He pulled me into a hug, and I reciprocated, watching Madison from over Cade's shoulder. She was playing with her hair, looking anywhere but us.

"We are going to be Anglerfish together."

As I pulled out of the hug, I gave him a scowl. "Don't say that. It sounds weird."

"I know. I know. Atlanta have the worst sports names. I mean, seriously, at least we aren't on the baseball team. The Atlanta Armadillos is definitely worse."

Cade was talking and I was nodding along, pretending to listen, but I was just watching Madison.

"We're going to need to get out of here and celebrate."

"Not tonight, man. I'm going to head home so I can tell my dad in person."

"Understandable, but you don't think he's checking?"

"He's at work. He won't have time, and he promised to let me tell him myself."

"Wish I could be there to see his face. He's going to be so happy for you. You've come a long way in the last eight years since I met you. I'll never forget watching your tiny ass flailing around on your skates while those idiots pushed you around."

"Apparently, you're never going to let me forget it, either."

Cade elbowed me and pointed. "Gotta make sure you remember when your loyalties lie." I couldn't help it, my gaze flicked to Madison, because he was right. My loyalties were with Cade. They always would be. "Still can't believe this happened for us."

"Neither can I."

Cade's dad squeezed his shoulder, drawing his attention away from me. As I stepped a little to the side, I bumped into Madison, who gave me a brief look before dropping her gaze to her purse and rifling through it.

She pulled out her phone, I couldn't help but be intrigued. I glanced down and just so happened to have the perfect view of her phone screen. Even when she turned a little to the side for privacy, my height made it easy to see what she was doing.

She pulled up her messages, and that was when I saw her texts.

Kyle: Madison, you're a really great girl, but I'm sorry. I think we can only be friends.

Mhm. Interesting. He listened, and I proved myself right, yet again. None of these assholes were willing to fight for her, ergo, none of them were worth her time. I couldn't help but smile because Kyle was officially leaving Madison alone. No one was going to touch my girl.

Fuck. She wasn't my girl. But at least she wasn't wasting her time with an idiot like Kyle.

Madison let out the tiniest of whimpers, still staring at her phone screen. I didn't like it because it sounded too much like she was upset again.

"What's wrong?" I asked, brushing my arm against hers to get her attention.

She quickly turned her phone screen off and stepped to the side so she could look at me from over her shoulder. Fuck. Her big blue eyes were dark, and her teasing smile had fallen. She was upset. Over another idiot guy, and I've already broken my vow never to see it happen again.

Was I always going to be the one that had to stand back and watch her get her heart broken?

"Nothing." She shook her head. "Just read a spoiler for a new show I've been watching."

Lies. All lies because she clearly didn't want to admit how she was really feeling.

Henry's behavior has broken her, and I just made her feel worse because

I forced Kyle to stop talking to her. I had mixed feelings. I didn't want to see Madison upset, but I was also happy that Kyle wasn't going to go anywhere near her.

"MB. Are you ready to come out and celebrate with us?" Cade asked as her parents smiled at her. I could feel her unease from here, but no one else seemed to notice.

"If you're tired, I can always take you home?" I offered and gave Madison's mom a small smile.

"Uh, yeah. I'm pretty tired. I think I need to go home."

I bit back my smile because I didn't want anyone to see this as anything other than a offer of a ride home.

"Are you sure you don't mind dropping her off?" Their dad asked.

"Absolutely fine. Your house is on the way to the firehouse anyway. I'm guessing my dad will still be there."

"Ever the gentleman. Thank you, Dash." Cade's mom pulled me into a hug. "And congratulations. We're all so proud of you," She said as she patted me on the back.

I hugged her a little tighter than necessary because I felt her words deep in my chest. I hoped I'd made my mom proud too.

By the time I was rolling up to Madison's house, she was fast asleep in the seat next to me. Somehow, she'd managed to curl herself into a ball and her head was resting in my direction.

Even asleep with her mouth hanging open, I couldn't help but think she was beautiful.

"Madison," I said lightly, hoping to coax her out of her sleep gently.

When she didn't respond, I nudged her shoulder.

Still nothing.

The girl was out like a light, and I considered driving straight to the firehouse and leaving her here.

But that didn't feel right. So instead, I opened my door, made my way around the car, and opened hers.

Ever-so-gently, I unbuckled her seat belt and slipped my hands under her legs and behind her back. Then, I hauled her into my arms and shut the door with my foot.

The thump of the door shutting, woke her up.

"What the fuck? Where am I?"

"Don't scream," I grunted, walking her to her door at pace.

"Dash. Where are we?"

"Your house. I'm walking you in."

"I have fully functioning legs you know?" There was a hint of amusement in her voice, and I was happy that she was seemingly no longer upset about Kyle.

He didn't deserve a minute of her unhappiness.

"Has anyone ever told you that you can sleep through a heavy metal concert?"

"Oh, please. Don't try to make out that you listen to anything other than sad, depressing music in your car. How could I not fall asleep through all that moaning?"

"Good to see you're fully awake now."

I bent my knees, ready to deposit her on the floor, but she wrapped her arms around my neck, and pulled herself into me.

"What are you doing?"

"What are *you* doing?" she retorted.

"I was going to put you down so you could walk the rest of the way."

"And I've never been carried like a princess before, so I'm more than happy for you to take me to my room like this."

It was a joke. She was just joking, and I pressed my lips together to look unbothered by it. I'd never been to Madison's room before, and the idea of waltzing in there to put her on her bed was taking my thoughts to places it shouldn't be going.

"I'll take you to your front door. That's it."

"Deal."

She rested her head against my chest, and I found myself slowing down because, for some reason, I wasn't looking forward to putting her down. Maybe her fruity shampoo was going to my head, and I was slowly losing my mind. I wasn't sure, but I also didn't care all that much because the stairs were looming in front of me.

"I could stay like this all day," Madison hummed. I looked down at her, and she had this small, placid smile on her face. I didn't want to take my eyes off her, but if I wanted to get to the stairs uninjured then I needed to.

She moved a little, forcing my fingers to flex against her thigh.

"Has anyone ever told you that you've got big hands?"

"Madison."

"What?" She opened her eyes, and tilted her head so she could look me in the eyes. "I guess it's not really something that someone would bother to mention because it makes sense. You're a goalie, so I guess you need big hands for that too, right? To catch the puck?"

"We wear gloves. I'm not out there catching the ball bare handed."

She snorted, and when I looked down at her, she quickly looked away.

"Sorry. Just something about the way you say bare handed. I don't know? It's just funny."

She was babbling and although I needed to keep up the façade of hating it, I loved it. Her thought process was cute, and there was something endearing about how open she was with me.

"You're also a big guy. How tall are you now? Seven foot?"

"I'm six foot six."

"Close enough," she mumbled before looking around. We were close to the steps now, and I was preparing myself for letting her go. Not just dropping her off at the steps, but leaving her behind. College was a few weeks away and I wasn't going to be able to see her anymore. It was a reality that I just started to accept.

"You're view is so different from up here. Is it weird to see so many scalps in the day?" I didn't answer because she didn't give me time. Gasping, she glared at me with the utmost seriousness. "Dash. You'd tell me if I had dandruff, right?"

My brows crossed, but she was looking at me so fiercely, I felt the need to respond with a shake of my head.

She breathed out. "Thank goodness. I don't think I'd be able to live that down, otherwise."

"Are you drunk?"

"No."

"Why are you babbling?" I asked, just as I let her feet drop onto the porch. Her arm stayed wrapped around my neck and when I glanced at her, I couldn't help but stop. We were so close physically right now, and I didn't want it to stop.

Her eyes were wide when she said, "I don't know. I guess I just talk a lot when I'm nervous."

"What's making you so nervous?" I almost whispered as I stood beside her, my face still close to hers. If I wanted to, I was close enough to kiss her.

Damn, did I want to. She was right there. Her mouth was parted and her big bottom lip was just asking for it.

But I couldn't.

I wouldn't.

"I, uh, don't know. Maybe it has something to so with being carried home by one of the most gorgeous guys I've ever met."

Did she just say that, or was I delusional?

Swallowing, I stood straight. Away from her lips and any temptation I had.

"You're home now," I said and cleared my throat. "I'll text your brother to let him know."

"That's it?" She said, looking hurt.

I averted my gaze to the floor because I couldn't look at her anymore. Too sweet. Too perfect. Never meant to be mine.

"I'll see you around." Even though I was still staring at the floor, I could feel her heated gaze on me, but I chose to ignore it.

A couple of seconds went by before she tutted. "I didn't realize you were such a coward, Dash."

With that, she turned on her heel and opened her door.

I stood there, feeling like a chump, slightly confused because I wasn't sure if She's just confessed her interest in me too, or if I completely misread the situation.

All I knew now was that I was standing outside my best friends house, staring at the door because I missed his sister.

What the hell happened to me?

Madison wasn't for me. She was going to be here for the foreseeable future, and I couldn't betray Cade like that. Not after the way his parents took me.

I couldn't break her heart, and this little obsession had to stop.

Nothing was going to happen.

It never could.

I stuffed my hands in my pockets as I headed to my car. Only three more weeks until I was off to California. I could handle seeing Madison until then. I just couldn't be left alone with her again because my brain did stupid things when we were alone.

As I opened my car door, I took one final look at Madison's house, noticing her purple curtain twitch. Was she watching me?

I shook my head because I shouldn't care about the answer to that.

So instead, I repeated the mantra in my head.

Three more weeks.

Three more weeks, then I was gone.

That should get her off my mind.

To Be Continued….

Read the rest of Dash and Madison's story here:

Want to read more about Tiff? Start here:

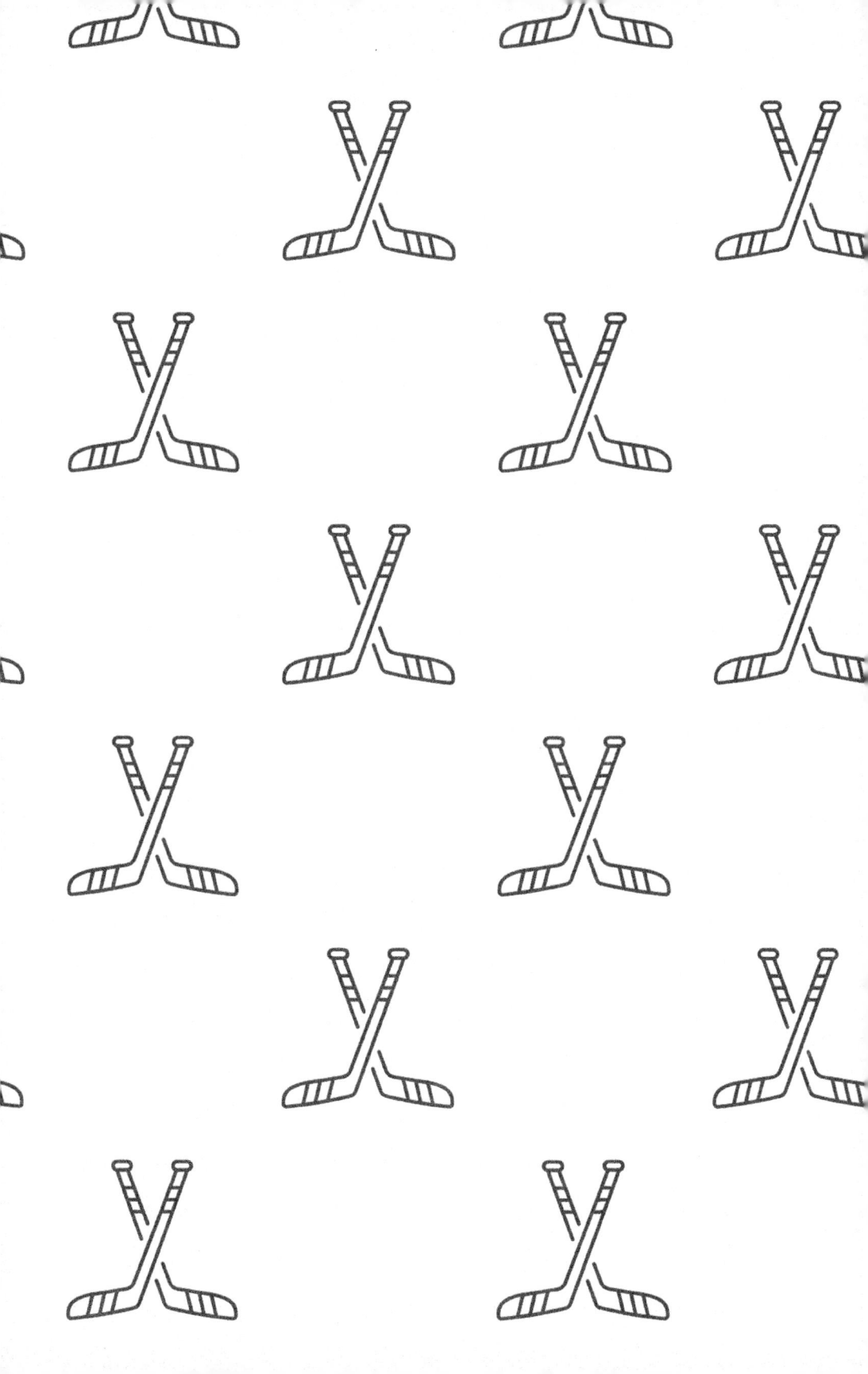

Printed in Great Britain
by Amazon

45807753R10046